License to Rule!

Princess ID card

Princess _____

from the royal kingdom of

_____

Birth date _____

Daughter of

King _____

Queen _____

POCKET Doodles For Princesses

ANITA WOOD
DRAWINGS BY **JENNIFER KALIS**

GIBBS SMITH
TO ENRICH AND INSPIRE HUMANKIND

Manufactured in Altona, Manitoba, Canada in
February 2012 by Friesens. Tracking # 72167

First Edition
15 14 13 12   15 14 13 12 11 10 9 8

Published by
Gibbs Smith
P.O. Box 667
Layton, Utah 84041

1.800.835.4993 orders
www.gibbs-smith.com

Cover designed by Melissa Dymock
Interior designed by Renee Bond

Gibbs Smith books are printed on either recycled,
100% post-consumer waste, FSC-certified papers
or on paper produced from sustainable PEFC-
certified forest/controlled wood source. Learn
more at www.pefc.org.

ISBN 1-978-1-4236-1877-5

This book is dedicated to Tammi, Sammi, Emalee, Mazie, Kiarra, Lizzy & Crystal—just a few of the princesses in my life.
Be loyal to the royal! —AW

For Elliot, my little drawing buddy.
—JK

"I am a princess. All girls are. Even if they live in tiny, old attics. Even if they dress in rags, even if they aren't pretty, or smart, or young. They're still princesses. All of us. Didn't your father ever tell you that? Didn't he?"

—Sara Crewe from *A Little Princess*, Frances Hodgson Burnett

You live in an Enchanted
Kingdom. What is it called?

Design a smashing pair of magical glass slippers!

Draw your own wishing well.
What would you throw into it?

You've been put into a
deep enchanted sleep.
What magic words wake you?

Draw an enchanted cottage
where everything comes
to life, even the dishes!

Draw some of the enchanted
dishes, spoons and cups.
Are they happy?

There's a dreary old dungeon in your castle. What would you expect to find there?

You have to spin straw into gold
for a crabby little old man.
What does he look like?

Where is your Winter
Palace located? Draw it.

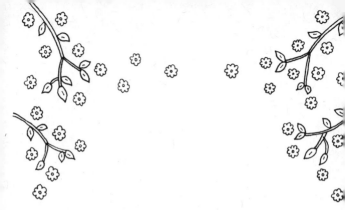

Time to move to your Spring
Castle in the meadowlands. Draw it.

What does your Summer Castle
look like and where is it located?

Fall is just around the corner
and your Autumn castle awaits
you. What does it look like?

What is the best thing about your royal BFF?

Decorate your dream princess bedroom.

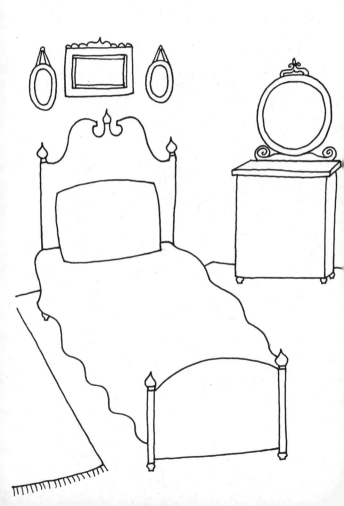

Add flowing curtains and
lots of pillows to this bed.

Design a sparkly lamp
for your bedroom.

A frog or a toad—which one makes the perfect prince?

Give your frog prince a
comfy lily pad to rest on.

Pucker up! You just kissed a frog.
Did he turn into anything?
Draw him here.

The frog you just kissed turned YOU into what?

You've fallen down a rabbit hole.
Where did you land?

What is in your royal jewel box?

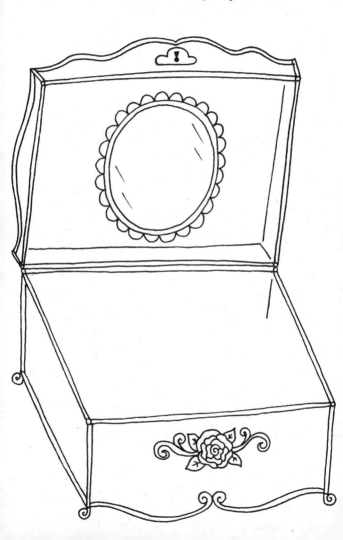

What does your everyday crown look like?

Now draw the crown you wear on special occasions.

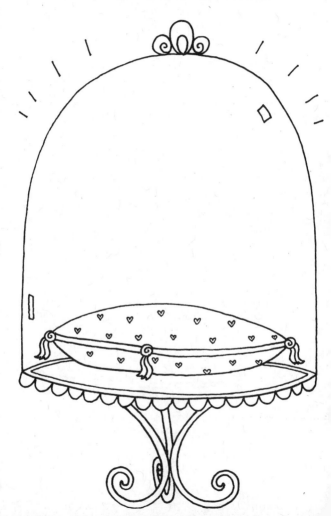

Design a crown for your Daddy, the King.

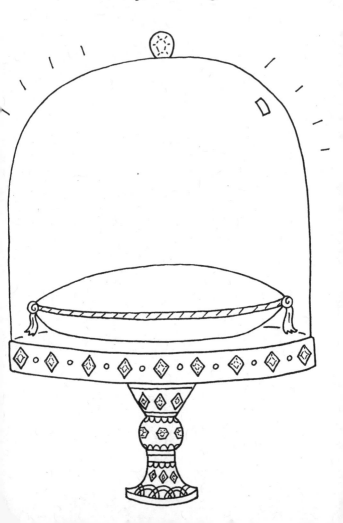

Design a crown for your Mom, the Queen.

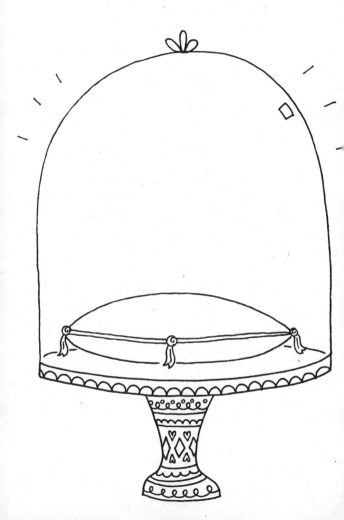

Princess Bride

Draw your dream wedding gown & veil here.

Icing on the bride! Create your sparkly tiara and matching earrings here.

Wedding ring bling!

Don't forget the fancy wedding shoes! Glammed up sneakers or satiny slippers?

Arrange your wedding bouquet.

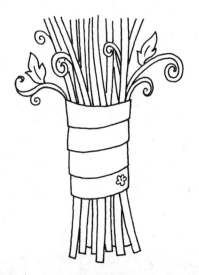

The Royal Wedding announcement. Write it here.

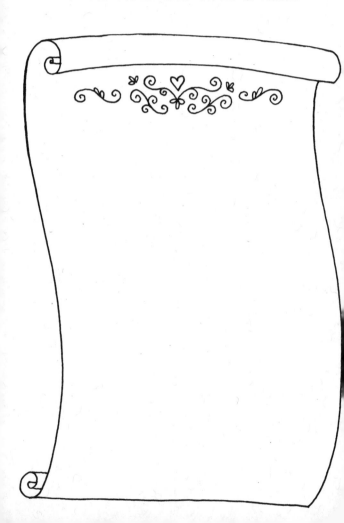

Going to the Chapel of Love!
Draw your wedding chapel here.

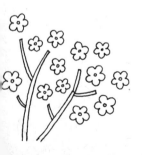

Put your own design on the wedding cake.

Design a special gown for the
princess Masquerade Ball.

Make a fun mask to
wear at the ball.

Her Royal Highness
princess stationery. Put your
design on this paper.

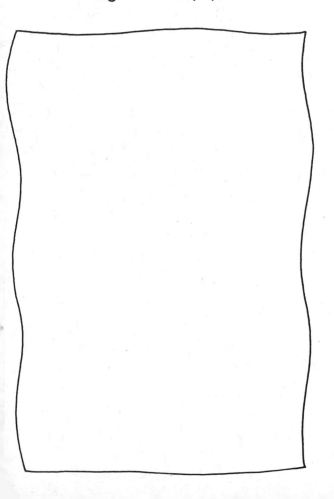

Design your own royal seal.

Give the royal pooch & kitty
their own glamorous outfits.

Design a royal sleeping place
for your princess poodle.

Design a princess carrier
for your pampered pet.

Draw your royal family portrait
here. (Stick figures are okay!)

Woodland Princess

Decorate this dress with pretty leaves & berries.

Draw some of your forest friends.

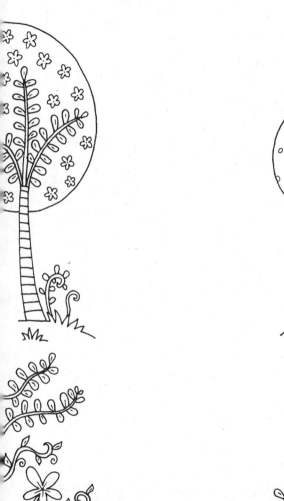

An old witch lives in the forest.
What does her hut look like?

Fairy Princess
Design a fanciful fairy dress.

Draw some magical toadstools
that house little fairies.
Maybe we'll see one!

This little doorway leads
to an enchanted fairyland.
What does it look like?

Design a pair of lacy
fairy princess wings.

Every fairy princess needs a
special wand. Finish drawing one
here. Don't forget the Fairy Dust.

Give the little fairy a flower skirt and hat.

Miniature fairy fashions. You've found some little fairy outfits hanging in the hollow.

Arabian princess

Draw a fun outfit complete with a short blousy top and harem pants.

Design some bindi dot jewels to wear between your eyebrows on special occasions.

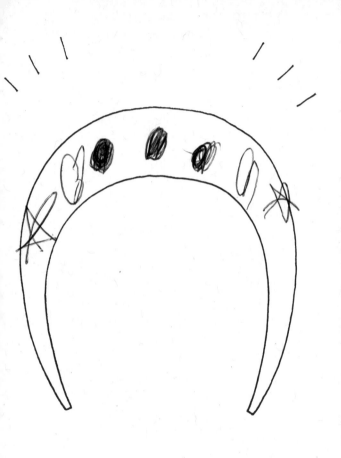

Create a jeweled headband to
wear when you visit the Sultan.

What kind of exotic pet would
an Arabian princess have?

Draw a magical design on this flying carpet.

You just freed a genie from the
lamp. What does it look like?

You are the genie princess inside
a magic bottle. What does the
bottle look like on the outside?

What does your magic genie bottle look like on the inside?

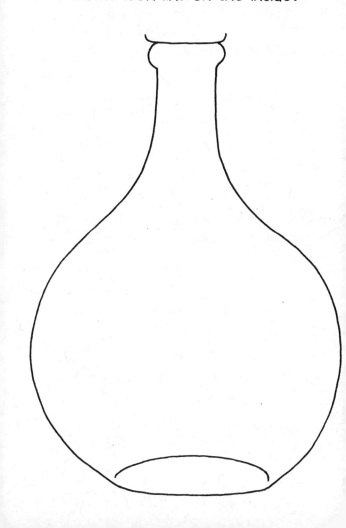

Native American Princess

What is your Native American
princess name?
Butterfly Cloud, Pink Moon?

Home Sweet Home.
Decorate your tepee so everyone knows a princess lives here.

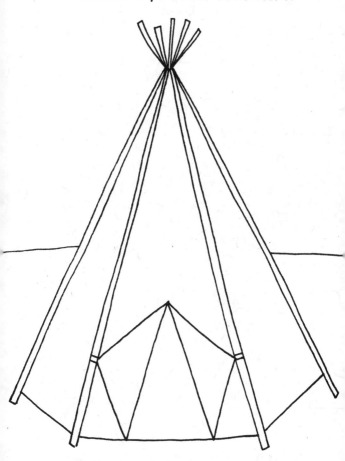

Decorate a deerskin dress &
leggings fit for a princess.

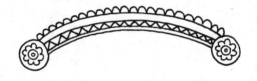

Make a feathered
hairpiece to wear.

Draw a beaded and fringed
bag to hold your treasures.

Design a fancy turquoise necklace and earrings.

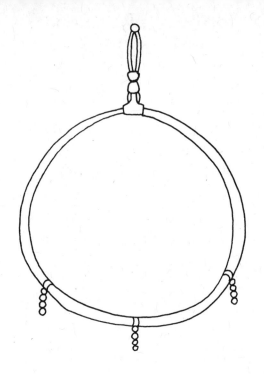

Finish this dream catcher to let all
of your good dreams pass through.

What is your animal spirit guide?

Magical Mermaid Princess

Give her some shimmery
scales and a cute bikini top!

Make a necklace & matching earrings out of seashells.

Design a pearl-studded tiara.

Draw some of your gill-friends.

Make a cute saddle for
your princess sea horse.

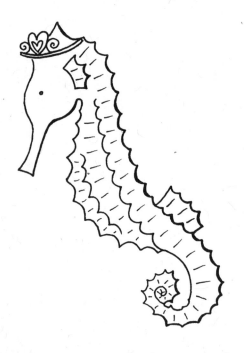

What does your underwater kingdom look like?

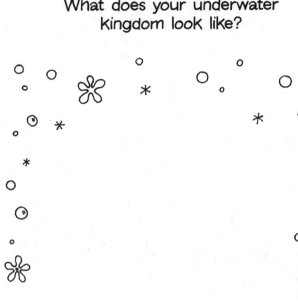

What kind of sea treasures have you collected?

Your bed is a huge clamshell.
Decorate it with some seaweed
curtains and puffer fish pillows.

Egyptian Princess

Draw a pyramid-shaped playhouse.

Mummy and Daddy have given
you matching arm bracelets.

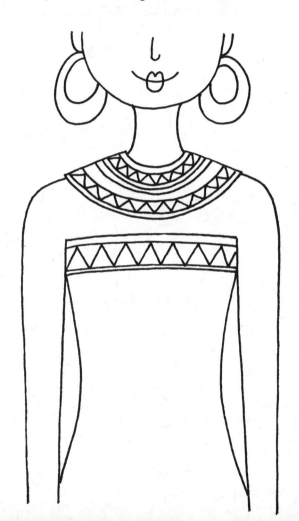

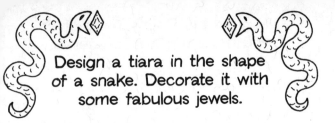

Design a tiara in the shape of a snake. Decorate it with some fabulous jewels.

Egyptians worshiped cats. Draw a friendly feline and name her.

Oriental Princess

Put a design on this kimono
fit for an empress.

Make a fabulous green jade necklace to match your outfit.

You have a pet panda.
What does it look like?
What is its name?

You found a beautiful lotus
blossom to adorn your hair.
Add it to this comb.

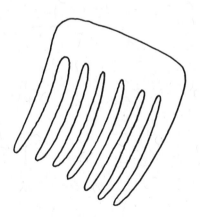

Put some fun designs on these paper lanterns.

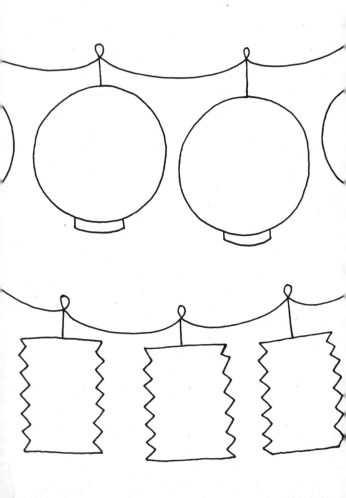

Decorate the chopsticks with
some dangling beads to make
a fancy hair ornament.

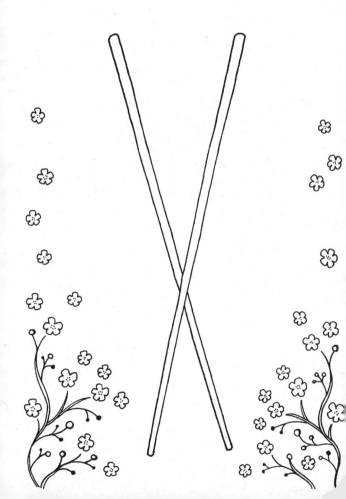

Spanish Princess

Ole! Design a colorful
multi-tiered dress.

What does your lacy fan look like?

Add some bright paper flowers to this vase.

Draw a birthday piñata. What kind of candy have you filled it with?

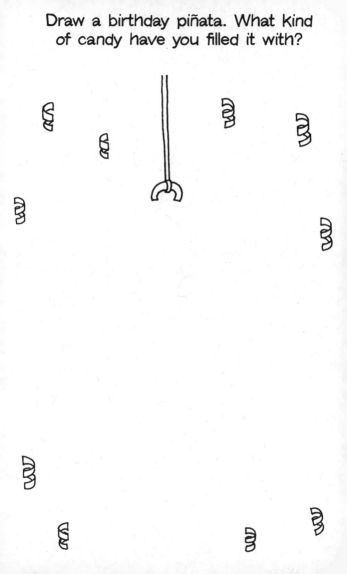

Butterfly Princess

Decorate the dress with
all kinds of butterflies.

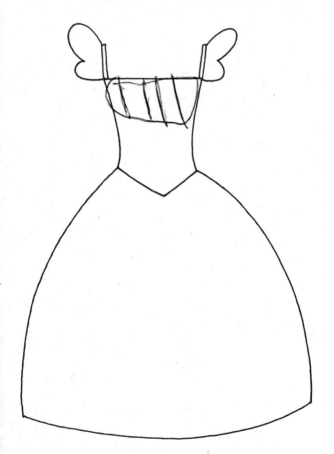

Butterfly princesses live in
lovely little houses that look
like flowers. Draw yours.

Flower Princess

Design a summer gown using
your favorite flower petals.

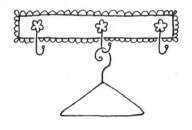

Put some pretty flowers on
this wreath for your head.

Make some dainty slippers
to match your dress.

Doodle your flower princess name here. There are lots to choose from. (Lily, Rose, Violet, Pansy, Holly, Rosemary, Daisy, Viola, Flora, Iris, Jasmine, Petunia, Heather)

Flower Babies

Draw a sweet little face on the rose.

Draw a puckered face on the pansy.

Draw a tiger face on the lily.

Draw a funny face on the sunflower.

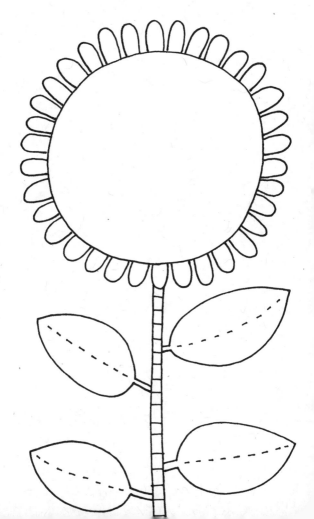

Rodeo Princess

Design a cute outfit with lots
of fringe and sparkle!

Frost your cowgirl hat with
a rhinestone tiara.

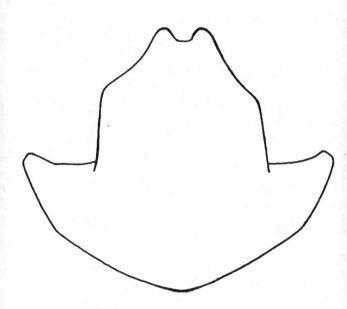

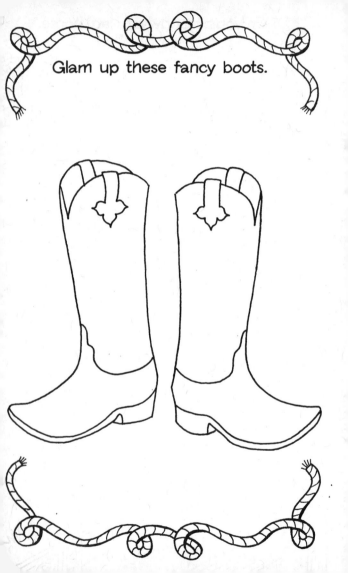

Glam up these fancy boots.

Draw your trophy-winning horse.

Pirate Princess

Design a cute sailing outfit.

Draw your pirate ship here.
What have you named her?

Put a design on your
princess pirate flag.

Add hands to this magic
compass that will guide your
ship to a fabulous treasure.

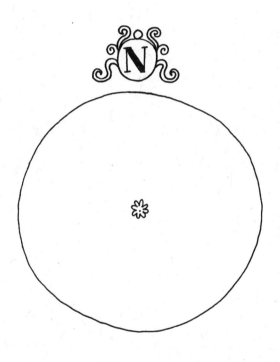

What is in the treasure chest?

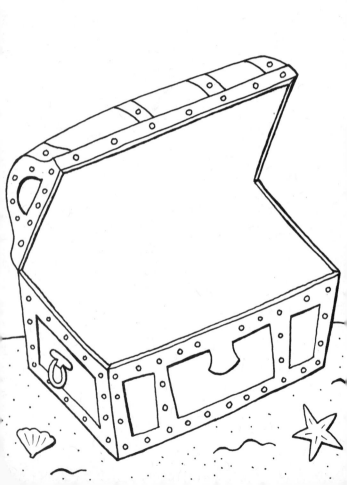

What else do you find on Treasure Island?

Snow Princess

Design a glittery gown.

* * * * * *

Design a snowflake tiara
& icicle earrings.

Create a sleigh to take you around your ice kingdom.

Make a fancy fur coat and hat to keep you warm.

Mod Princess

Design a cute tiara to go with
your favorite pair of jeans.

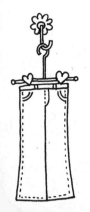

What will you wear to
the Royal Prom?

Decorate this fancy pair of high
gloves to wear with your prom dress.

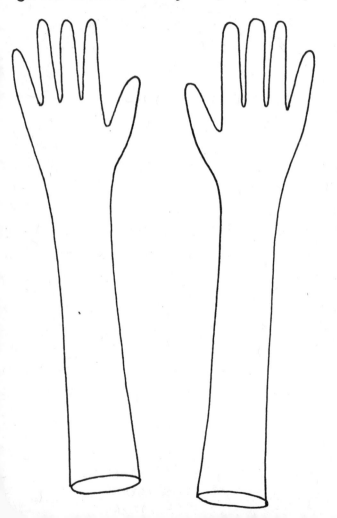

Draw your dream limousine.

Beach Princess

Design a fun little bathing
suit & cover-up.

Every beach princess needs a
sandcastle. Build one here.

Fantastic flip-flops! Design a pair.

Design a pair of starry-eyed princess sunglasses.

Tea for two—you and your BFF.
Draw a teapot and a cup
for each of you.

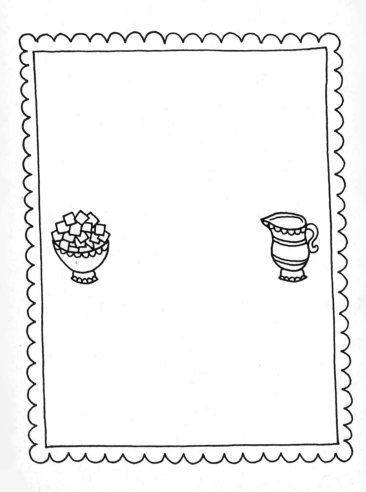

Royal Feast.
Set the table with golden plates
and bejeweled cups and bowls.

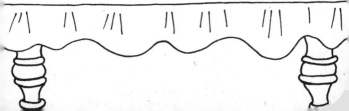

Who is your knight in shining armor?

Happily ever after. Where is yours?

Happily Ever After...

Princess maze.

START

Find your way to the castle.

Who is your favorite fairy-tale princess? What do you like best about her?

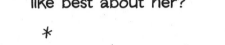

Who is your favorite fairy-tale prince? What are the qualities that make you like him?

What is your all time favorite
book about princesses?
Draw a cover for it.

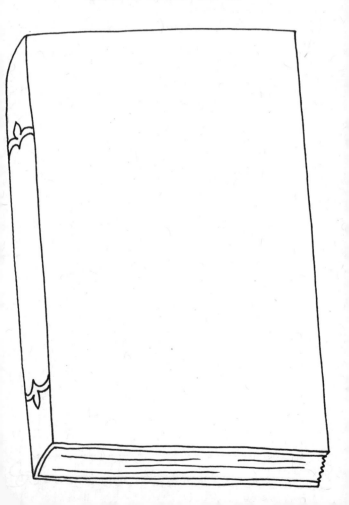

Princesses love pink!
Draw a picture using your
favorite shades of pink.

Every Ballet princess needs a
lovely pink tutu. Design one here.

Who would you put a love spell on?
What magic words cast your spell?

Your prince used to be a scary
beast. What did he look like?

You've been locked in a tower
waiting for your true love to
rescue you. Finish the tower.

What is the name of your sweetheart prince's horse? Draw the horse.

A gypsy fortune teller just read your palm. What did she tell you?

She said...

_____

_____

_____

_____

_____

_____

You are throwing a party for all of your friends. What will you serve?

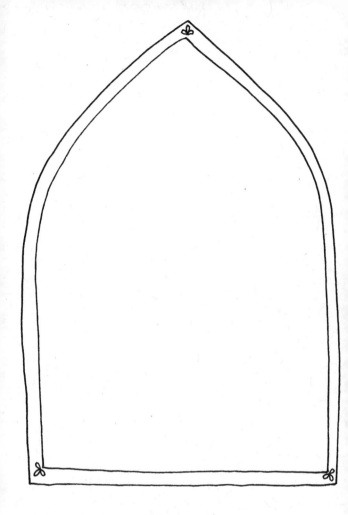

Draw a stained glass window
that tells a story.

What is growing in the castle garden?

When you're not wearing a princess gown, what's your favorite outfit?

You've followed a rainbow to its end. What treasure did you find there?

Draw the cover of your princess diary.

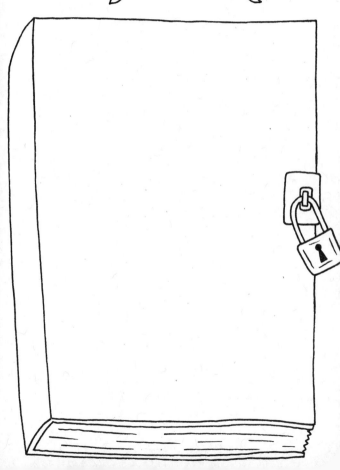

Draw a feather-topped pen to
write your fabulous secrets with.

My Secrets...

Create a stylish hair-do on
this sweet princess.

Design some sparkling hair
accessories to wear.

Add some ribbons and
roses to this headband.

A wacky old wizard lives in this tower. What does he look like?

What does your princess throne look like?

Camping in royal high style!
Draw your tent.

Princess picnic—pack the basket with all kinds of goodies.

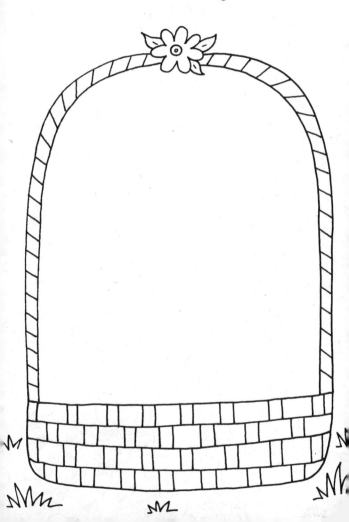

The trees in the Forbidden Forest are magical and can talk.
Draw one of them.

Design a frilly cape to wear on a cool spring evening.

Super Princess!
What are your special powers?

Draw a princess action figure doll that looks like you.

It's all about the accessories!
Design a purse that will
make your friends jealous!

You have your own princess money.
Design your bills and coins.

Miss Princess Pageant

Design your winning gown
along with your sash.

If you won the pageant, how would you use your princess title to help others?

Parade Princess

Draw your float here.

Design a big floating balloon for the parade.

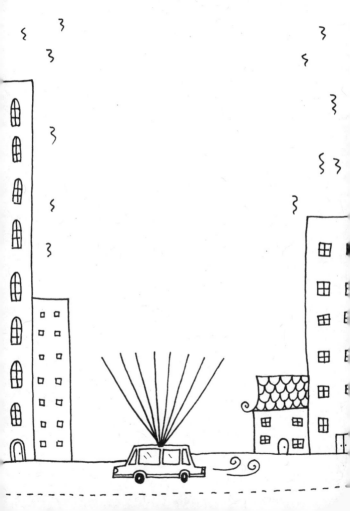

Sweet Princess

Decorate the dress with candies.

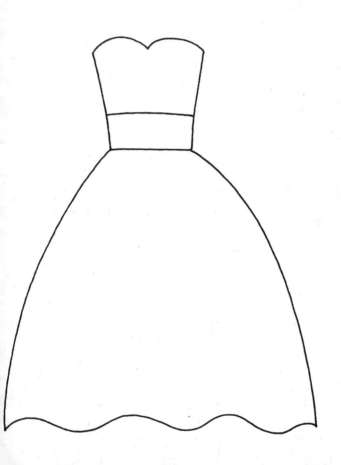

Princess Sweet Shop serving ice
cream sundaes. Draw them here.

You've just wandered into
the Lollipop Forest.
What does it look like?

Every sweet princess needs her
own Peppermint Palace.
Draw yours.

Fill the sky with fluffy marshmallows and cotton candy.

A giant and his family live
in a nearby cave.
What do they look like?

Give yourself a princess pedicure.
Draw a cute design on your toes.

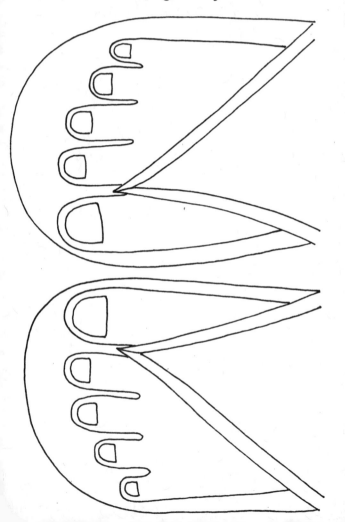

You've just eaten an apple that
is full of a sleeping potion.
Who gave it to you?

Princess Dreams—what's the best one you've ever had?

Some of your best friends are little people. Draw their cottage here.

Sprinkle some fairy dust and other decorations on these cookies.

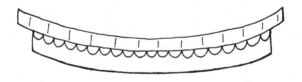

Design a fountain to go in
front of your palace.

The Princess Times. Write a headline about you!

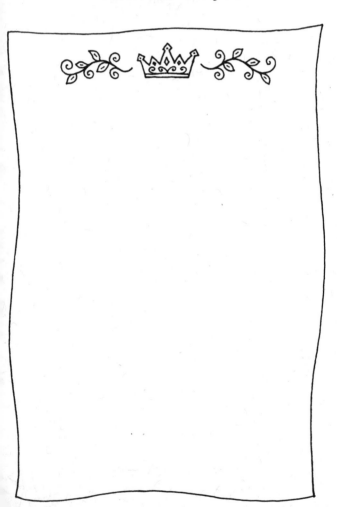

Sharing secrets with your BFF.
What are they?

A special holiday celebrates you!
Mark your day on this
calendar and decorate it.

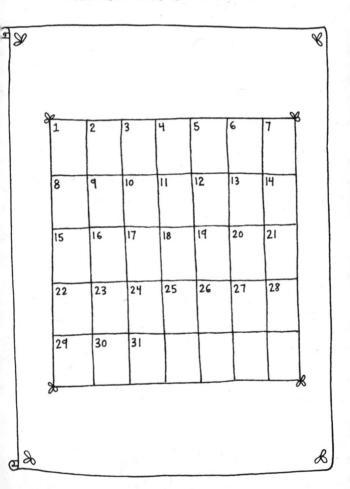

1	2	3	4	5	6	7
8	9	10	11	12	13	14
15	16	17	18	19	20	21
22	23	24	25	26	27	28
29	30	31				

Draw your favorite princess PJs and slippers.

Design a bottle for your favorite perfume.

A day in the life of a princess . . .
What do you do?

You are a tiny princess and live in
a dollhouse. Fill it with furniture.

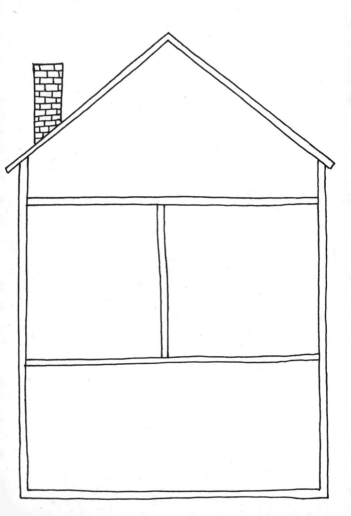

You fly from place to place
on the back of a dragonfly.
What does it look like?

Princess ABCs

A is for Angel, Apple

B is for Bling, Butterfly

C is for Castle, Carriage, Crown

D is for Diamond, Dragon

E is for Emerald, Elf

F is for Fairy, Frog

G is for Godmother, Gown, Gold

H is for Heart, Horseshoe

I is Ice-cream, Icicle

J is for Jewel, Journal

K is for King, Knight

L is for Love Letter, Locket

M is for Music, Magic

m

N is for Necklace, Nail Polish

O is for Ogre, Ornament

P is for Pearl, Pony, Party, Prince

Q is for Queen, Quilt

R is for Ruby, Rose

S is for Slipper, Star

T is for Tiara, Troll, Throne

U is for Unicorn

V is for Veil, Valentine

W is for Wand, Witch, Wizard

X is for Hugs & Kisses

Y is for Yellow, Yes! (what you say when asked to the dance by your crush!)

Z is for Zoo, Zippity-doo-dah

Princess dress-up. Does your mom have a dress that you would love to wear?

Bewitched! Princess by day and what by night?

Princess birthday party. What would you put in the goody bags for your guests to take home?

Decorate your "Sweet 16" birthday cake.

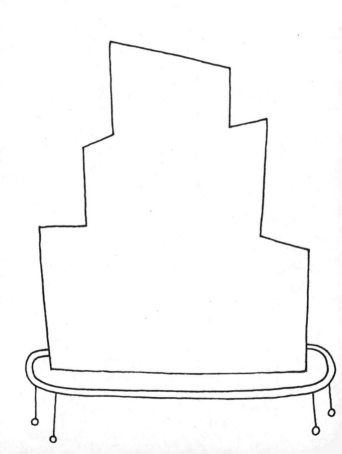

You're invited...

Make your special birthday
party invitation.

Who are the other
princesses in your life?

Rockin' Princess! Draw your band's
name on this set of drums.

Turn this pumpkin into
a fancy carriage.

You are Beauty. What does Beast look like now that he's changed?

Decorate your cell phone
with some glittery jewels.

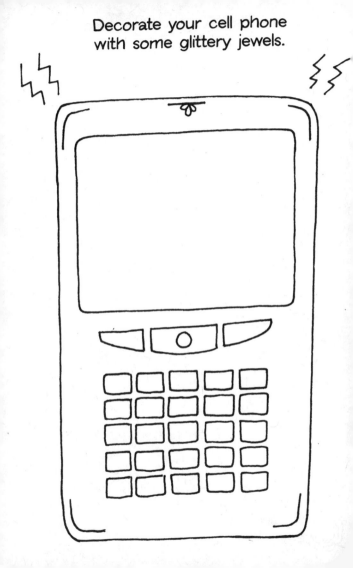

Princess daydreams. Where does your imagination take you?

You have your own line of princess
chocolate candies. Design a
cute box to package them in.

Five things you love about
being a princess.

Ruling in style!
Design your royal scepter.

Princess Club. Design a piece of
jewelry to be worn exclusively
by you and your girlfriends.

What does your clubhouse look like?

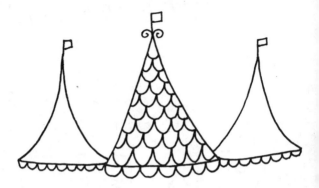

What fairy tale characters do the following people remind you of?

MOM

DAD

SISTER(S)

BROTHER(S)

BEST FRIEND

TEACHER

What fairy tale character would you be? How would you change the story?

{Character}

{Before}   {After}

Who are your ladies in waiting?
(best girlfriends)

Dreams do come true if you believe. What is one of yours?

Princesses LOVE to shop! Where would you go on a free shopping spree? Draw your purchases.

Give this carousel horse a
fancy paint job and some
flowers in its mane.

Valentine Princess

Design your romantic gown
for the Sweetheart Dance.

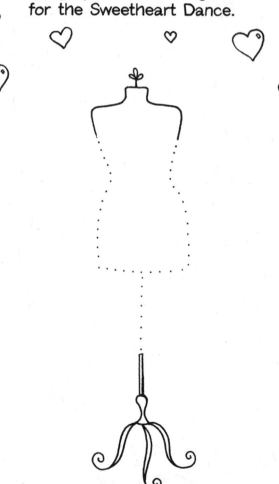

Make some heart jewelry
to complete your outfit.

You have a magic closet that produces anything you want to wear. What does it hold?

Have a magical day! Describe
the best day you can imagine.

My best day ever would be...

Garden Princess

Design a pretty dress using frilly lettuce leaves and make accessories from other vegetables.

Design a cute tea set
using daffodils for cups
& sunflower saucers.

Design some Ladybug earrings to accessorize your garden outfit.

Dragonfly hair clips would add
the perfect touch to your "do."

Design a lacy spider web cape
to go with your garden gown.

A daisy chain crown would
top off the whole look.

Fill the lantern with some cute little fireflies.

Are you more of a princess or a queen?

Define your inner goddess
and draw a picture of her.

Build a fancy pink
lemonade stand here.

Mirror, mirror on the wall—
draw an elegant one here.

Decorate these cupcakes.

You join the circus as the "High Wire Princess." Draw a cute costume for your daring act.

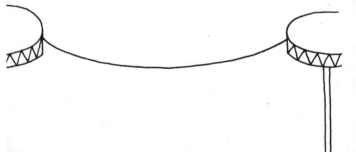

Make a fancy carnival mask to hide your secret princess identity.

Draw your favorite stuffed animal.
Does it have a name?

Decorate the princess hat.

Draw a dancer inside
this music box.

There's a storm outside, but those aren't raindrops! What is falling?

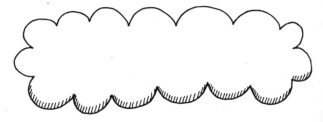

The brightest star in the sky is
actually the Star Fairy. Draw her.

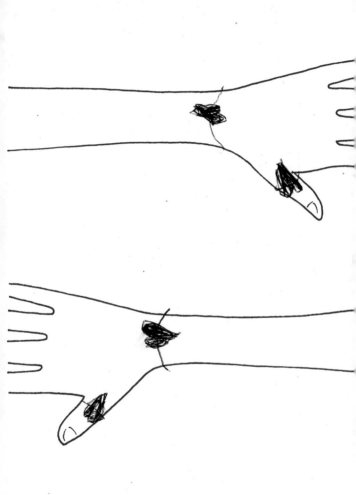

Friendz 4 ever! Design matching
bracelets for you and your BFF.

Create a cute bottle that will hold some magic pixie dust.

Pretty as a princess—that's you!
What do you like about yourself?

1

2

3

4

5

List 5 things someone would put in a trap if they wanted to catch you.

1. _____

2. _____

3. _____

4. _____

5. _____

Create a princess charm bracelet
with these charms: crown,
slipper, ring, wand, heart, star.

Decorate the unicorn with
magic flowers and glitter.
Give her a name.

You just slid down a rainbow and
landed in an enchanted valley.
What did you find there?

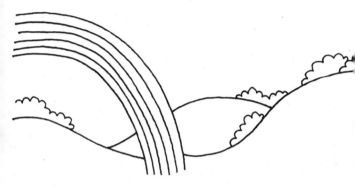

You've been gathering berries to
make a pie for your prince.
Fill the basket.

Songbirds wake you up each
morning with happy tunes.
Draw the little music makers here.

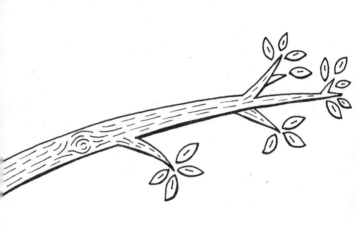

Design a playhouse where you can play make-believe with your friends.

Design a ring for each finger.

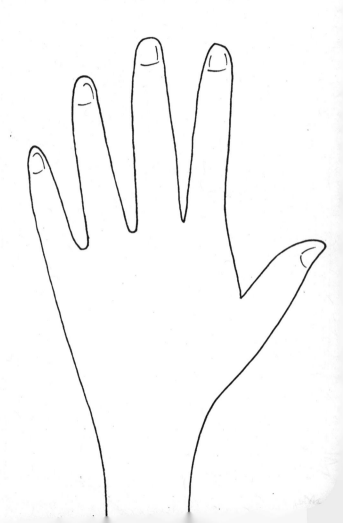

What do princesses carry in their purses?

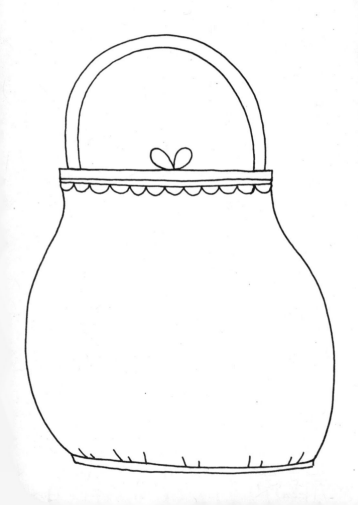